MW01298027

A System of Legal Logic: Using Aristotle, Ayn Rand, and Analytical Philosophy to Understand the Law, Interpret Cases, and Win in Litigation (A Scholarly Monograph)

RUSSELL HASAN

DEDICATION

Dedicated to every soldier who ever gave their life to fight for the United States of America

CONTENTS

ACKNOWLEDGMENTS

I would like to thank my professors at Vassar College and the University of Connecticut School of Law, as well as all the philosophers whose work inspired this book.

1 THE PAPER: A SYSTEM OF LEGAL LOGIC

This paper begins with a glossary of philosophical terms and then applies them to construct a system of legal logic. The system of legal logic presented herein will go a good way towards introducing much-needed clarity and precision in how lawyers and judges think about the law. To the extent that everyone is governed by a legal system, it is also good reading for everyone (although a high intelligence and knowledge of the law, and a background in philosophy, may be required to grasp the academic legal details).

T: a Thing, a set of properties, can also stand for one isolated property.

X: an X, a T as the object of analysis.

p(T): a perceived T. The object.

P(T): a perception of T. The means of perception.

W(T): a witness of T. The subject.

e(X): the essence of X, the property from which X derives ontological being as X, what makes X be an X.

S: specific properties nonessential relative to an essence.

>: the arrow of inference, which indicates that the content on the left side evaluates to the content on the right side by a direct inference of reasoning.

X minus S > e(X).

R(X): a real X. An X which exists in Reality.

p(X) > X.

X = S plus e(X).

Therefore p(X) > e(X).

p(R(X)) > R(X).

E(X): the essential thing X. A T which lacks S and lacks R and has only e(X).

C(e(X)): the consequence of the essence of X. Those properties which e(X) will cause T to have.

XY: a T which has the property of being X and the property of being Y (i.e. X times Y). For example 2 x 3 is the number two having the property of being in a set of three: XX + XX + XX = 6.

The Essential Syllogism: $e(X) > E(X) > C(E(X)) > C(e(X))$.

The Essential Argument: if a Thing must have the essence of X in order to be an X, and having the essence of X causes a Thing to have the property Y, as a consequence of the essence of X, then all X are Y, because being X causes T to be Y, therefore each X is Y, therefore all X are Y. It is necessary and universal that all X are Y if you can establish a "because" relationship between $e(X)$ and Y. If a critic asserts that some X is not Y then if it had the essence of X this would cause it to be a Y because it was an X, therefore it is not an X after all, because it lacks $e(X)$, or else it would have been Y if it had $e(X)$.

The Empiricist Argument: if a thinking entity can gain knowledge of X from $p(X)$ and gain knowledge of $e(X)$ from X and gain knowledge of $C(e(X))$ from $e(X)$ then there exists the possibility of a posteriori knowledge of necessary and universal truth, arising from the empirical perceived immanent ontology of things, not from the mind imposing categorical conditions onto subjective experience.

The Objectivist Argument: that the means of perception do not create or bias the act of perception, that $p(T) = T$ and $p(T)$ causes $P(T)$. Therefore we see and experience objective reality, and the phenomena are the noumena. The argument holds that $p(T)$ cause, are prior to, and exist separately from and independently of $P(T)$, that we see $p(T)$ by means of $P(T)$ but the T we actually see is $p(T)$ and $R(p(T))$, whereas $P(T)$ exists in our minds (actually as nerve signals in our optic nerves and brains).

The Closed Eye Argument: that from perceiving something, then not perceiving it, then perceiving it again, one can infer that it existed while one was not perceiving it, therefore it exists objectively, and from this one can infer $R(R)$, that Reality is real.

The Painted Box Argument: assume a box with each side painted a different color. Four people on four different sides look at the box. Each sees a different color, but each side is the color that is seen, so all four are objectively correct, and their perceptions are not subjective. For each side $R(p(T))$ therefore $R(Sum(p(T)))$.

The Color Blind Argument: that color blind people see less of Reality, not a different Reality. For example purple equals red times blue so if you see both blue and purple as the same color you see blue but only the blue part of purple.

The ABC Principle: $C(e(ABC)) = C(e(A)$ and $e(AB)$ and $e(ABC)$ and $e(B)$ and $e(BC)$ and $e(C)$ and $e(AC))$

b/c: because.

Non(X): Not X, a Thing is not X, or lacks the property of being X. If Q is X was asserted as an assertion this means that statement is False, it is not

True.

N: the number in a series of a potentially infinite set.

The CD Principle: e(ABC) > D, e(ABNon(C)) > Non(D), either C > D or AB x C > D.

r: Reason, especially Essential Reasoning. The substantive analysis of why e(X) causes Y. Always reduces to a b/c relationship, that X causes Y physically, Y is a part of X in other words X contains Y e.g. X = ABCY, or X requires Y as X's means or the cause of X where Y is the only possible cause of X. Must be done at the level of specificity of the subject matter, e.g. philosophy for e(T), chemistry for e(water) > becomes ice when freezes, that case's specific evidence for a trial.

K(T): to know T. Semantically identical with: to believe R(T).

Conceptual Identification(ConID): p(X1) > (X = e(X) + S(X1)) > e(X) > E(X) > C(E(X)) > (C(e(X)) = Y) > (p(X2) and Non(p(Y))) > K(X2 = Y). To reason that all X are Y, see an X but not see Y but know that Y is present despite no empirical direct evidence. The basis of analytical philosophy as logic.

The Blue Green Fallacy: inferring that all X are Y from repeatedly seeing XY without r(b/c), i.e. without establishing a because relationship between essence and consequence.

The Lab Rat Fallacy: X is an M, Y is an M, scientist establishes all X are Z and asserts all Y will be Z because of M, and then a Non(Z)Y is discovered and it looks like r is not necessary and universal, but in Reality X was Z because of S(X)M so not all Y are Z.

The Black Swan Fallacy: the definition of the word W is commonly known, all W are Q, but then a Non(Q)W is found and it seems logic teeters, but it turns out that W had two meanings(M): T1 and T2 which are found together 99% of the time but only all T1 is Q and this was a Non(Q)T2. Which definition is correct? Actually it is best to coin one W for T1 and a second word W2 for T2. S is always relative to e(T) so this will produce the correct C(e(T)).

The three consequential mechanisms:

Cause: the essence directly causes a thing having it to have the consequence because of what it is.

Contain: e.g. being B is a consequence of being AB.

Means/Effect: the essence requires the consequence as its means of being or the consequence is the only cause of that essence as its effect.

The 99% Rule: 99% of the time there is no practical difference between being 99% certain or 100% certain. For example the extent to which you Know that the Roman Empire existed because a big lie about it is too implausible.

C%: degree of certainty.

TR%: degree of trust.

C% = TR% + K(C(e(X)) + p(X).

How to prove a negative: prove all X are Y, Y is not Q, therefore all X are not Q, not Q is proven.

The Space Time Statement: R(T) = (R(T(S(location)) + R(T(S(time))).

R: Reality. (Intentionally uses the same letter as R the property of being Real.)

Metaphysical Possibility (Meta Po): that T is possible in theory, that the nature of R allows it, that no essence to consequence relationship contradicts it.

Mechanical Possibility (Mech Po): that R(T) is possible, that the physical means of R(T) does in fact exist, that T is possible in practice.

Ignorant Possibility (Ig Po): that we do not know (1) if T exists or (2) if T is metaphysically or mechanically possible so (3) we say T might exist.

PW: the Physical World.

Descartes' Demon and Hume's Darkness (DDHD): Skepticism, the belief that Non(R(PW)) is possible, that the physical world might all be an illusion and we cannot prove that the Sun will rise tomorrow morning.

R(R): that Reality is Real.

R(PW) that the Physical World is real, which may imply R = PW.

Valid and Invalid Possibility Inferences:

Valid:

Meta Po from Mech Po,

Mech Po(T) from R(T),

Non(Ig Po(Not(T))) from R(T).

Invalid:

Meta Po from Ig Po,

Mech Po from Ig Po.

The Anti-Hume Postulate: that it is invalid to infer that T is possible from imagining or conceiving of T.

The Anti-DDHD Argument: if in the first instance you can affirmatively infer empirically from p(T) that R(T) therefore R(Sum(T)) therefore R(PW) and from this infer Non(Ig Po(Non(R(PW)))) therefore Non(DDHD). Also if C(e(PW)) > R(PW) then Non Meta Po Non(R(PW)) therefore Non Ig Po Non(R(PW)) > Non(DDHD).

The Objective Relative: the theory that a measurement of X in relation to Y is objectively true, not Subjectivist or relativist, if R(X) and R(Y) and R(X/Y).

SOM: Standard of Measure. The T in relation to which X is measured.

The Aristotle Caveat: A cannot be Non(A) at the same time and in the same respect, but can be in a different respect, meaning in relation to a different SOM or as a different essential property.

Paradigm: a very broad doctrinal or mindset-level SOM.

If (A + B = C) and (R(A) and R(B)) then R(C).

If p(T1) > T2 > T3 > TN then R(TN) b/c p(R(T1)) and R(T1) > R(T2) > R(T3) > R(TN).

If (p(A) + B = C) then R(C) only if (p(B) or p(T1) > R(TN) > R(B)).

I(X): X is irrational, meaning K(X) but Not r(X). X is irrationally believed.

If (A + B + C = D) and (p(A) and r(B) but I(C) then Ig Po(D). D may or may not be R. If in the next step r(R(C)) then r(K(R(D))).

Pure reason (Pure(r(X)): Reason only from perceived things or conclusions validly drawn from them, with no irrational premises.

The Purity Postulate: that perfectly pure reason admits of 100%C because R causes P which causes K(R(T)). Impure logic should not be trusted until all premises are empirically verified.

Scientific Experiments: ((IV + Cf) = DV) = (X – S(X) = e(X) > C(e(X)))).

IV: independent variable.

DV: dependent variable.

Cf: confounds.

PA: patterns in data.

SIG: statistically significant patterns in data. To the extent that a SIG DV is found and all Cf are not causing it, because they were controlled for and their effects were subtracted out, it must be caused by IV because there is nothing else there to cause it and it was SIG hence not just random, therefore DV=C(E(IV)).

Statistically significant conclusions based on random samples admit of the degree of certainty of its probability but only up to 99%.

The Essential Argument of cause and effect of essence justifies the necessity of the If Then statement in formal logic.

X = ABC, p(AB), is it X? Is AB enough for X? Only up to 99%C from circumstantial evidence. The more important thought in that scenario is C(e(AB)). If that cannot answer the question then Ig Po(X).

The Essential Thing Method: if you can assert Y of E(X) then it must be C(e(X)) because there is no S there to cause it, there is only e(X) there present to cause it.

The Aristotle Method: the essence of X is that thing which when removed does not leave behind that thing of which it was the essence, so to find the essence conceptually remove properties from a Thing until you would no longer regard it as an X.

The Philosophy and Law Postulate: the Law is applied philosophy.

The Legal Logic Postulate: the Law defines an act Y that the government will take if a judge finds that Facts F are equal to X, therefore L is the statement Y because X, therefore the Law defines the legal consequence of the essential properties of a set of Facts.

F: Fact or Facts.

L: the Law or laws.

RA: the Rationale of the holding of a judge in case law, which states why he held as he did, i.e. X b/c Y.

Elemental Logic: breaking F into T and matching them up to the elements of a claim in L. A process of Legal ConID of identifying a set of F(T), breaking L into a set of e(T) where C(e(T)) = the desired legal outcome, and matching the properties in T to e(X). To match all elements is to state a claim, to prove all F(e(L)) is to prove your case.

EL: an element of a claim of L. An EL is an e(T) where L = (O = C(e(EL))).

O: outcome, what the government will do if a set of R(F) satisfies L(EL). The goal of a lawyer is the client's optimal or desired O.

Statute: legal text defines L = e(X) explicitly, or you infer using canons of statutory construction and definitions.

Common Law: opinion says L = T b/C RA, you must infer e(T) from RA.

Max C%: the maximum potential r(L)C%. Unless the Law and its definitions are perfectly explicit and clearly define L, the Max C of L is 99% or less depending on how clear L is. For a multifactor balancing test with high judicial discretion, Max C%(L) might be 1%. Max C%(F) = the degree to which the consequence of the essence is proven from p(T) of every EL, which can be 100% or the lesser degree of TR% of circumstantial evidence.

The burden of proof: a definition of Min C%(minimum degree of certainty) to prove that all facts necessary to prove all elements of a claim are proven.

Max C%(Case) = Max C%(L) + Max C%(F). The opposite of it is DDHD(Case).

The Prediction Postulate: All X are Y is the basis of the belief that K(L) enables predictions of future O where future F = X2 given future F because L = e(X) where FN = (X + FN(S)).

Making the Pro Argument:

Step 1: p(F1) or p(T) > r(T) > r(TN) > F1 (prove the facts).

Step 2: EL1 = e(X) (interpret the Law).

Step 3: F1 = EL1 (the facts satisfy the elements of the Law).

Step 4: repeat for FN = ELN (the facts satisfy all elements needed to win).

Step 5: O = C(ELN) (win the case and be awarded the desired outcome).

Answering the Con Arguments:

Assume case law is one case such that:

Holding = L1

Facts = F1 + F2 + F3

Rationale = RA1

Your client's Facts are F4 and F5.

You want L1 to apply to your F.

You argue:

(L1 = e(F1) b/c RA1) and X = e(F1 as L1) therefore X = EL1, and F4 is a type of X (is of the category of X) because $F4 = e(X) + S(F4)$.

This is your Analogy: F4 is like F1 in the way significant to the Law as shown by RA1.

Opposing counsel's arguments are Distinction:

F1 is not $e(L1)$, instead F2 is EL1, and F4 plus F5 is Not $e(F2)$.

$EL1 = F1 + F2$ and $F4 = F1$ but F5 Not $= F2$.

$S(F4 + F5)$ adds something that blocks $C(e(X))$ because of RA1.

Non(F4 or F5).

$F4(SOM)$ Not $= X(SOM)$.

DDHD. C% or TR% is too low.

In plain English: EL requires F not present here to be met, you are wrong about which facts in the opinion are legally significant, you are wrong about what was the essence of the legally significant fact, you misread the Rationale hence the previous two counterarguments, the specifics of the facts in your case change the legal significance of your facts matching the essence of the case law's facts in a way indicated by the case law rationale, the essence are not the same because you use a different paradigm to interpret and analyze your facts than the case law used, you failed to prove your facts even if your elemental logic was correct. You did not prove knowledge of the facts sufficient to meet the burden of proof against skepticism of your facts.

You then reply to each counterargument by making the Pro argument directed at it.

Analogy: these facts have the same essence but different specifics as the legally significant essence defined by the facts of case law or the definitions in statutes.

Distinction: the essence is different.

Horizontal counterargument: you say X, I say Not X.

Vertical counterargument: you say X, I say Y (and If Y Then Not X).

The Philosophical Rule of Evidence: the goal of evidence at trial is 100% Certainty. This explains the demand for firsthand testimony and authenticated evidence sufficient from which to infer each element of a claim, and other things, such as the rule against hearsay. It is an Empiricist philosophy that all knowledge must originate in direct perception and then be logically inferred from that.

Authenticating Evidence: establishing the Purity of the line of reasoning from perceived things (firsthand evidence) to the conclusions. The chain of custody of evidence shows the decision-maker a basis to trust the line from $p(T)$ to $K(F)$. Hearsay and the other rules of evidence are based in the principle of Pure reason that all conclusions must ultimately be based upon and grounded in $p(T)$. If $p(TN)$ can be introduced into evidence and proves F as a consequence of the essence then C% can equal 100%, otherwise C% is limited to TR% of circumstantial evidence from which to infer F. Tangible physical evidence that judge or jury can see for themselves can be 100%C, otherwise where a Witness W testifies that she saw T this can be like p(T) for the line of r but is limited to TR%(W).

The Closed Eye Method: prove objective R(T) by corroboration or that T existed between periods of being perceived as T is asserted to be.

The Painted Box Method: explain away differing accounts as different POV but all consistent with the underlying R(F).

The Color Blind Method: explain away differing accounts by deficiency in POV, means of perception, P(T), compared to the ideal perfect POV that saw your asserted F.

To extend the analysis of law by philosophy and logic, let us ask this question: Can we derive the Law conceptually and analytically from the analysis of concepts?

H: the property of being Human.

R(H): a real person, a realistic person as analyzed by logic.

X: a person. (X = E(Human)).

A: a second person. (A = E(H)N/X).

X/A: the relationship between X and A.

What is C(E(X/A))? What political relationship emerges between X and A from nothing other than their essence? What conditions must be met within X/A for a specific politics to arise?

POLI = C(e(X/A)).

How does POLI define the Law or limit the scope of possible Laws? What conceptually understood contingencies cause a Law potential in a POLI to collapse into an actuality?

A thought experiment is relevant here in order to answer the preceding questions. As a theoretical challenge, let us ask, and answer, this question: can Libertarianism be justified pragmatically using a priori logic? If so, how and under what conditions?

A priori: from before, from the analysis of concepts without reference to empirical research.

Pragmatic: practical, justified by its usefulness and benefit to real human beings.

Assume a thought experiment:

X is a person.

A is another person.

Y is X's belief, what X believes is good. A believes Y is evil.

B is A's belief, what A believes is good. X believes B is evil.

Assume X and A are members of one political system.

Assume these possibilities:

1. X can let A be free to do B.

2. A can let X be free to do Y.

3. X can impose Y onto A by force.

4. A can impose B onto X by force.

5. X can fight in self defense against #4 but cannot stop A from trying if A wants to.

6. A can fight in self defense against #3 but cannot stop X from trying if X wants to.

Game Theory Question One: given this hypothetical, can we infer all possible scenarios and rank them from the a priori point of view, in other words, before we know what Y and B are and which is good and which is wrong? Do we have sufficient information to do so?

Scenario One: #1 and #2. Freedom and peace between X and A. X happily does Y and A happily does B, marred only by each's knowledge that somewhere the other exists, to the extent each has a legitimate interest in controlling the other.

Scenario Two: #3 and #4, the war of all against all, the struggle for power, might makes right, the fight to seize control and impose your values onto the dissenting other.

Scenario Three: #1 and #4 which leads to either: 7. A defeats X and rules X or kills X or else it leads back to 5: X succeeds in self defense, which reverts to #5 but X can either maintain #1 or switch to #3 which becomes Scenario Two.

Scenario Four: assume #2 and #3, then either 8. X rules and conquers A or to #6 where A can continue #2 or switch to #4 which leads to Scenario Two.

Game Theory Conclusion One: Scenario One is the optimal outcome because X is able to do Y and A is able to do B and every other outcome entails greater risk of one or both of these conditions failing but the game theory shows that X and A cannot force each other to resolve to Scenario One. X can try to give #1 to A in return for #2, and A can give #2 to X as payment for #1, a reciprocity of freedom, and this would be practical from a pragmatic a priori point of view of before we know who X and A are, what position on which issue Y and B are, or even whether X likes or hates A personally or vice versa.

Game Theory Conclusion Two: any #3 or #4 leads to scenarios where a Scenario Two outcome is more likely: the slippery slope.

Now with the basics under our belt let's explore more variations of this game.

Assume this argument: X says he should force Y onto A because he would let A force Y onto him in return or as payment or for fairness.

Posit this counterargument: the equivalent of X's Y for A is B, not Y, so if X tries to force Y onto A the reciprocal or fair and equal outcome is for A to force B onto X.

Assume the following argument: X is a crusader for justice who believes Y is good and B is evil so wants to escalate to Scenario Two and win the war.

Posit these counterarguments: from the a priori point of view X does not know who will win the war so in this "from before" perspective it maximizes the chances of the maximum existence of Y and minimizes risk of loss of Y to choose Scenario One, and this is true even if X firmly believes B is gruesome horrific evil because this is a pragmatic argument to maximize Y. The only objection is the extent to which B's very existence injures X but we can isolate these into moral revulsion, which is merely an emotion that can be ignored as the price one pays to coexist in civilized society, or a physical intrusion of B into X's moral space, which would theoretically revert to X's right of self defense in #5 and the path back to #1 and Scenario One.

Now it's time to assess decision-making authority and its allocation. Assume these possibilities:

9. X decides between Y and B for X.

10. A decides between Y and B for A.

11. X decides for A between Y and B.

12. A decides for X between Y and B.

Note that any attempt to escape this question by removing an option or choice from its scope reduces to #11 or #12. For example to say "we will give X only B and remove the possibility of Y so there exists no choice nor decision to be made" is logically equivalent to "A chooses B for X."

Game Theory Question Two: can we infer the logical result of all possible scenarios and see what this fact pattern evaluates to given the postulate that we do not know a priori the intelligence, IQ, knowledge, expertise, education level, ignorance or lack of knowledge or lack of wisdom of X and A? What possibilities does this set resolve to?

Scenario One-a. #9 and #10. This is the epistemic corollary of Scenario One.

Scenario Two-a. X seeks, or achieves, #9 and #11, which, if X chooses Y for A, as X probably will, leads to #3, then Scenario Two.

Scenario Two-b. A seeks or achieves #10 and #12, leading again to Scenario Two.

We can deduce that as a practical matter #9 and #10 maximize Y because they avoid Scenario Two and thereby protect and guarantee at least X's Y while leaving open the possibility that X may persuade A as decision-maker for A to freely choose Y over B as a result of reasoned dialogue and persuasion.

Assume that:

13. The decision of Y vs B for X impacts only X.

14. The decision of Y vs B for X impacts X but also affects Y.

15. The decision of Y or B for A only has a result or effect for A.

16. The decision of Y or B for A had results and effects for both A and X.

If #13 and #14 are true then we may say that Scenarios One and One-a meet the condition of being fair and just: X bears the result of X's choice, A takes responsibility for the decision for which A is responsible. However it is also logically true that #15 and #16 are not incompatible with Scenario One and One-a if, and only to the extent that, X if #16 asserts #5 and uses force for self-defense to the extent necessary to protect himself from intrusive impacts of A and #10, and the same for A that if #14 and 9 then #6.

The Libertarian Assumptions:

The First Libertarian Assumption: assume that there is no difference between social conduct or economic conduct, beliefs, religions, morality, behavior, what to say, think, or do, or plans for how to manage the economy or distribute resources or assign productive efficiency, in terms of what substantive content can be plugged into the variables Y and B.

The Second Libertarian Assumption: in the state of nature X and A can (a) delegate their right of self-defense to the government or (b) delegate their war to impose Y or B onto each other to the political process so that the war of bloodshed becomes a war for votes to elect politicians who will impose either Y or B onto the public.

From this we can assess a certain set of policy questions:

Let the individual or the government decide what an individual can do with his property and money?

Let individuals or the government decide the banking interest rate?

Let the individual or the government decide how much of his money to spend on social causes or charity for the poor (taxes)?

Let the individual or the government decide which medical treatments or medications he can or can't use (FDA)?

Let the individual or the government decide to what extent a person may harm his own body (recreational drug use, obesity-causing food, the legality of suicide for the terminally ill, etc.)?

Let the individual or the government decide whether he (and by extension his religious sect) should recognize gay marriage as legitimate?

Let the individual or the government decide whether she should have an abortion?

Let the individual or the government choose what he is allowed to say (free speech vs libel laws)?

Let the individual or the government decide whether to recognize immigrants as members of his social and political community?

Let the individual or the government decide the terms of the individual's economic interactions with foreigners and trade across borders?

Let the individual or the government decide what religion he is?

Let the individual or the government decide with whom he does business, whom he sells to, buys from, hires or fires?

Let the individual or the government decide with whom a person can interact socially, whom they can date or marry and on what terms (the terms of a marital relationship, the legality of prostitution, Jim Crow-era racial segregation where the government forced whites and blacks to be kept apart, etc.)?

Let the individual or the government choose his or her healthcare?

Let the individual or the government choose their children's education?

Game Theory Conclusion Three: In the classic game of game theory, the prisoners' dilemma, two prisoners are separated and may confess or lie. Their benefit is maximized if they both lie but because each can't force the other to lie they are both motivated to individually confess. This is deemed a collective action problem where the efficient solution is to force both prisoners to lie, which by analogy justifies the government to force citizens into behaviors to solve real large-scale collective action problems. With the XYAB game the problem is similar yet different: X and A cannot force each other into the optimal Scenario One given that the freely chosen non-violence and peace-selecting behavior of the other is necessary to achieve it. But because Scenario One entails freedom from government interference and political domination, it would also be difficult to solve this collective action problem by having the government impose it by force or by law. In an ideal outcome, the voters would freely choose Libertarianism, having been persuaded in their capacity as decision-makers. The next best thing is for the law to assign decision-making authority for each individual to that individual, to enable each person to have a right of self-defense physically and/or legally, and to use constitutional law to safeguard the rights of the individual against the tyranny of the majority. However no system can render Scenario One fully necessary as a result of a political system because it will always rely on the contingent free choices of X to choose #1 and of A to choose #2.

This system is self-validating: a libertarian wants to be free to make his own decisions but will not impose his values onto others by force, so he would let someone else be free to oppose libertarianism and be an adherent of tyranny and an enemy of freedom, but the libertarian would not let his enemy impose his tyranny onto the libertarian by force.

The XYAB Thought Experiment neatly translated into the common law:

(1) X decides for and has decision-making authority and freedom individually for his life, liberty, body and property.

Let LLBP be defined as Life, Liberty, Body and Property.

(2) Constitutional law: protect X from A imposing B onto X by means of votes and politicians, in other words, protect the individual from the government by creating a system of laws which the government is forced to obey. Protect X's LLBP from public intrusions.

(3) Criminal law: disallow A to violate X's LLBP by violent international force.

(4) Torts law: disallow A to violate X's LLBP by violent accidental force.

(5) Property law: protect X's LLBP from private intrusions, especially into X's decision-making authority, and establish rules to determine what is or is

not within the scope of X's LLBP.

(6) Contract law: establish rules for how X may trade parts of his LLBP in return for compensation, which, if based on X's freedom to make decisions, entails interpreting the intent of X in choosing the deal and what terms of the deal X intended to consent to, as well as whether X received the compensation which justifies assigning his LLBP to the other party.

(7) Due process: giving X the right of self-defense for his LLBP by giving him a hearing where he can legally put up a fight to defend his rights, and notice so that he can attend the hearing.

(8) Environmental law: prevention and/or compensation to the extent that A's pollution injured X's legitimate interest in his LLBP (and note that, if X's LLBP is legitimate, no huge amount of profit by A could justify violating it at a theoretical level, because it is a moral right prior to economics).

(9) Intellectual property: balancing the extent to which X gains LLBP by inventing or artistically creating inventions or works of art with the extent to which these do not physically exist and/or are preexisting things which are discovered, not created, and hence would fall outside the scope of X's LLBP as inventor or author.

(10) We conclude this section with a reference model mapping the scope of LLBP: 1. Self/mind/soul/consciousness, 2. Free will, 3. Choice, 4. Body executing choice, 5. Do work/make money/perform social behavior, 6. Actions go out into the World, 7. The economy, society, and other people interact, 8. The World sends the result of your chosen actions back to your body, 9. Your body receives the result and 10. The result is experienced by the self. LLBP covers the scope of the body as it expresses choices in such a way as to create property or relations which have a physical moral component of a result that impacts, rewards or punishes the self as decision-maker by the property and/or body receiving a benefit or detriment, liberty as the freedom for this moral lifecycle, and life as a self living in a body whose choices and actions create the sustenance (physical rewards) to keep the body alive.

This mode of thinking is useful for lawyers and helps make legal arguments. Consider the following questions:

Who is your client? Or, if you are doing policy advocacy, who is your stakeholder?

What was the scope of his LLBP? Where in the LLBP Lifecycle was it? From what source did it originate?

What choice did your client make? What was the result? What should have been the result?

How did the other party wrong your client? How was his LLBP violated? What choices gave rise to the conduct at issue? Who was responsible? How can they get what they deserve?

How did the other party disrupt your client's LLBP Lifecycle? How could the healthy circuit be restored? What damages would accomplish this?

Can the Law impose the result that would have resulted had your client been free to defend himself or been properly defended by the government as the agent to which he delegated his right of self-defense?

To what extent would it be wrongful or unfair had someone else done to the other party what they did to your client? This can establish wrongful conduct or doing the reciprocal back to the other party might be a measure of the fairness of damages.

Was your client's freedom impaired under the justification of protecting others? Can you make the pragmatic a priori argument that those third parties would benefit more from freedom for everyone than from this instance of protectionism?

We can analyze what might be called Scenario Two Law: a L designed to impose control or to collapse a law-abiding democracy into a dictatorship. X uses the government to impose control or grab decision-making power. By regime:

In torts, an excess of liability and litigation, to the point where ordinary people live in fear of the Law.

In contracts, the tyranny of fine print that nobody ever actually consents to.

In property, the replacement of inalienable rights grounded in human nature with a set of arbitrary entitlements arbitrarily assigned by society.

In environmental law, a takeover by regulators of all natural resources.

In intellectual property, a regime where our employers own our minds and owners censor and control our ideas.

In due process, the belief that the government can trample over us and crush us after notice and a hearing.

In constitutional law, the removal of all meaningful limits on government power.

$d(X = X)$: do the action based on X being X, treat an X like it is an X, behave in reaction to $R(T = X)$.

$d(X = Y)$: do the action based on X being Y, treat an X as a T of type Y, treat this X as a member of category Y, behave in reaction to $R(T = XY)$.

If (If X then do(Y)) then $Y = d(X)$. Belief X is the Premise of Action Y.

$d(R(X))$: behave as if X is Real.

$R(d(R(X)))$: the objectively correct way to behave as if X is Real.

$X(do(Y))$: X does the Y action.

$X(do(Y)while(Z))$: X does the Y action while Z is true or while the Z condition is met.

O+: a good outcome.

O-: a negative outcome.

Assume X is a hammer and Y is a pillow. If you try to build a house, and you use a hammer to hammer nails into wood, you can succeed. If you try to hit nails with a pillow, you will fail. You succeed by treating a hammer like a hammer in Reality. Conversely, if you try to sleep, and you treat a hammer like a pillow, and rest your head on it, you fail. If you treat a pillow like a pillow, you fall asleep by resting your head on the pillow. Treating a hammer like a pillow seems insane but the principle is real and widely applicable: do you treat yourself like the person you really are? Do you do the right things at work? Do you treat each person as who they really are? Do you treat politics and economics and laws as what they really are?

The R in d(R(T)) causes O+. If you do the right thing then you will do an action well and treating Reality like what it is enabled you to conquer Reality. In Law, treating the R(F) like what they really are will enable the truth to emerge before the jury, and treating each L as what it is will enable accurate legal reasoning.

J: the Japanese Distinction, which holds that Non(R(X)) is not equal to X = Non(T). To not exist is not the same as to not be something. T is to be something whereas R is to exist. (In English there is one word "is/to be" whereas the Japanese language has two distinct words.)

Objectivist Logic: the logic that follows from Non(J).

Objectivist Logic in sum: If(Not(1 < T)) then T = zero. If a thing is not something then it is nothing. If it is something then it is one with everything, lacking contradictions. This is true of TN so each T can never contradict a second T.

Objectivist Logic rejects J: to be something is to exist in Reality because 1=R, PW=1 and T=1, to be something is to exist is to be one thing is to be part of the one world that exists, to be a contradiction is to be two things at odds with each other or in conflict or where one severs itself into two so half can hide from the other half of the truth, therefore every T will integrate into R because they are already part of 1 thing and 1 is at one with itself so part of 1 cannot contradict 1 and R is 1 and all T are part of R therefore a contradiction cannot exist and the real will always integrate into Reality. Contra the reification of the zero, to think that something could be nothing, that a 1 could not exist, to be a walking contradiction or an irrational human.

<: the symbolic logical notation for the Objectivist Inference, that what is on the right side of the operand integrates into what is on the left side without contradiction.

K(PW) < p(T): the key Objectivist method of analysis.

Essential Logic: T > C(e(T)).

Objectivist Logic: 1 < T.

If (1 < T) and (R=1) then T/R: if a T is really something at one with itself then it exists in its proper relationship and ratio to Reality. Reason as a ratio of T to R.

If (Not(X < Y)) then Not X or Not Y.

Reason as the art of non-contradictory identification: integrate your sensory experience into your knowledge of reality. If it integrates without contradiction, then know it. If it resolves into a contradiction, a contradiction cannot exist therefore either K(PW) or p(T) is wrong. Think and look to the evidence you know is true to determine what the truth is and which one is true. Reality is one thing, it cannot be two at odds with itself, therefore a contradiction is impossible.

CONT: a contradiction.

To use some empirical examples from the Objectivist novel Atlas Shrugged:

In summary:

Rearden: ethics < sexual desire = CONT.

Dagny: Looter PW < p(Galt) = CONT.

Galt: Capitalist PW < p(20th Century Motor Co. socialism) = CONT.

The K(PW) or the P may be false but something must be true.

More detailed Objectivist examples from the Randian novels:

Howard Roark = Architect as 1. He has integrity to one principle: he will be true to the fact that he is (and wants to be) an architect, he is one thing with no contradictions.

Rearden: sexual morality as acceptance or toleration of evil < sexual desire for Dagny = CONT, resolved by reforming morality.

Galt: knowledge of morality and reason, that goodness must succeed because it is good < the sight of the Communists winning at the 20th Century Motor Factory = CONT, resolved by depriving evil of the permission of the victim.

Dagny: her worldview that the achievers and people of ability can save the world < Galt and the uncontrollable collapse of the world = CONT, resolved by accepting Galt's morality and the ideas in his speech.

These examples show that K(PW) or P(X) can be wrong when K(PW) < p(T). If it resolves to 1 then true, if it resolves to CONT then find your mistake and check your premises (question each of your assumptions and beliefs and the empirical evidence that gave rise to them).

The best method for executing Objectivist Logic: (K(PW) < p(T)) > If K(PW) then X > T=X or T=Not X.

< as Integrate: if X < Y then Y integrates into X without CONT. Then we can say INT(X < Y).

Integrity: INT(You < You(do(X))). The one principle that a T must be consistent and coherent with to have organic consistency. For example, for Howard Roark, d(You=Architect).

Politics: INT(H < POLI and Law).

The Objectivist Logical Argument of Politics: Assume you could choose either Y or B. If Y or B is True you need the freedom to reason which one and choose that one in order to survive, b/c d(R) = O+, and ultimately doing right or wrong leads to life or death. The moral and only the moral is inherently practical because d(R)=O+ and r is the means of K(R(T)), and since alive or dead are the only two contingent conditions for H and morality implies choice and free will it must be true that moral status is defined by which of life or death it achieves.

Objectivist Logic for Lawyers: view the case as 1 story where everything must fit in without CONT to make sense and CONT is a clue to a lie. View the statute or case as 1 and the legal interpretation that assimilates into it without contradiction and has integrity to the Law is true. So:

Case law < your reading of the law.

Statutory text < your legal interpretation.

Body of law or legal regime < your legal reasoning and paradigm.

Your case and its story < every fact.

Objectivist Logic values Integrity as the intellectual and philosophical foundation of reason. A lawyer whose reason and story of the facts of the case and legal analysis has Integrity is more trustworthy and credible.

Rational: resolves to 1, does not resolve to CONT.

If (X < Y) then XY is rational as a T or X + Y is rational as a whole or group of T or (if X then Y) or (if X then Po. Y) is rational.

Three key Objectivist concepts: integrity, consciousness, and the choice to think.

Integrity: to be one thing, to = 1(T), to be T as 1. To be true to one unifying principle of who you are("to thine own self be true".) R(H) as 1. Then, in epistemological terms, to integrate sensory experience into your previous knowledge without contradiction: epistemic integrity, that R = 1 and H(K(R as 1)).

Consciousness: the H as knower of R as 1. The mind as the thing that sees and reasons and integrates and chooses. Consciousness is the act of non-contradictory identification: the signature Objectivist epistemology.

The choice to think: because Reality exists objectively and is one thing, if you open your eyes then you will see it, and it defines you, and you plus Reality defines what you should do, and what you should do defines your choices, so your only really free choice is to open your eyes or choose to close your eyes. If you choose to think, your consciousness can and will reason from sensory experience to knowledge of Reality.

To blank out: to choose not to think. This involves splitting the one consciousness into two halves: the mind that knows the truth (inevitably), and the mind which hides from what it knows. What happens to James Taggart at the end of Atlas Shrugged is the horror of knowing you lied to yourself.

To apply this to lawyers: make your arguments as if the Judge is really very smart. If he is, opposing counsel will fail. If he isn't, you still look smart and may (and should) win. And the higher up the appellate court chain you climb on appeal, the smarter the judges tend to be. Really open your eyes and see the case, reason from the facts, know the law, and a winning argument (or the argument that should win even if it does not, which you can't help) will naturally emerge by applying the law to the facts with logic. The same with jurors, as at the end of The Fountainhead: treat the jury with intellectual respect, don't talk down to them, reason with their minds, and engage them cognitively. You cannot predict how a herd of sheep will stampede, so you may lose anyway if the jury is stupid, and therefore you have nothing to lose by making smart rational arguments to a jury based on reason and reality.

This paper offers a brief account of foundational bias. Foundational bias happens when a party at trial asserts that the other side is biased. If the other side makes a substantive argument or argues that they are not biased, both arguments can be dismissed as biased and therefore not credible. If your argument that you are not biased is itself asserted to be biased, it can become impossible to win the argument absent the tools of legal logic with which to defend yourself. To counter the assertion that X is biased when X asserts Y, X must do three things: assert Y, assert that he knows Y, and assert that it is possible for him to know Y. Further, if Y is factual and the asserted bias is some sort of subjectivity, X must not only assert Y but must also assert that Y exists objectively, that X knows this, and that X can know this. If Y is a legal interpretation, a lawyer must be ready to assert the degree to which it is knowledge and not mere opinion, and why and how he knows it. The lines of reasoning and methods of inference explained in this paper, and the relatively simple system of shorthand notation to organize legal logic, which can be used to diagram and explain proofs, can empower you to make each of the arguments that you need to make in order to overcome accusations of foundational bias, skepticism at its most fundamental, and to prove your case.

The Anti-Cogito Ergo Sum Argument:

Version 1: R(R)? = R() + R?, R() = R, if R then R(R).

Version 2: R(R?) = R(R or Not (R)) > R(R) and R(Not(R)) > R(R) = R and R(Not(R)) = CONT = 0.

Version 3: R? = R or Not R. If Not R then R(Not R) = CONT = 0.

In other words, to ask if reality is real, there must be a reality and real beings there to ask that question. If the question of whether reality is real is asked, the question is real, so something is real, so the real exists, so reality exists. If nothing is real then the question of whether reality exists is unimportant and the question itself is not real so there would be no doubting of reality absent that question so the question would not be asked.

The main application of this is to summary judgment (where a litigant can win without going to trial if there is no genuine issue of material fact for a jury to decide). If a real question exists, summary judgment should not be granted. If the only issue is whether to grant summary judgment then it should be granted. The Reality of the issue is what the inquiry should focus on: can R(F)? be asserted in logic without contradiction?

This section concludes with an account of de novo vs. clear error review and judge's discretion vs. mandatory outcomes and questions of first impression vs. stare decisis and binding precedent. Reasoning is a lot of work and the legal system only wants to pay for it once. If $F > r > L$ at the trial level, the appellate judge can review the facts to determine the correct outcome, or review the trial judge's reasoning, which takes the validity of his cognitive choices for granted, at which point he is just checking the structural soundness of the logic, whether it is logical, which reflects the clear error standard of review. The same is true of state decisis: the legal system only wants to do the work of spending money and costly doctrinal heavy lifting once. In questions of first impression or where a judge has been granted discretion by the laws he is technically unbound. But this account of freedom vs. mandate is deceptive. A judge has free will and can always do whatever he wants. In the case of A v. X a judge can rule for A or X at trial and a an appellate judge on a clear error standard can hold for A or X and can say any plausible analysis as his opinion. But Reality always defines one clear outcome, because the Facts exist objectively and the party who should win is defined by applying the Law to the Facts. Truth, justice, and $L = C(e(R))$ vs. Anything goes, the arbitrary relativist subjectivist stance that every position has pros and cons and you should just arbitrarily pick a position with pros you like and cons you can live with, is a dichotomy, essentially of free will vs. determinism and Objectivism vs. Relativism, that is true for every judge in every case realistically, regardless of binding precedent or standard of review. A judge should always pursue the Truth and hold according to Justice, and a lawyer can argue for truth and justice, instead of adopting the relativist stance that his job is merely to make arguments and the Judge can plausibly choose among positions from whichever pros take his fancy or cons don't dissuade him. R as $1 > L = 1$. If X then do Y, $R(X)$, therefore $L(do(Y))$. (X v. A(apply L to F)) $>$ (X or A) = rightful winner.

As some bonus content at the end of this paper, please enjoy this legal wisdom:

The law is opinion ossified into knowledge. So there are two types of arguments: the argument from subjective opinion, and the argument that old subjective opinions are knowledge that can't be questioned.

Lawyers are the guns of modern duels.

A lawyer is a warrior of words.

The law is common sense justified by obscure technicalities. So there are two types of arguments: the argument from common sense, and the argument from the obscure technicalities.

A lawsuit tells a story about right and wrong. There is only one winning argument: my client was a good person and the other party wronged him.

On any legal question there is always room for debate, but about this statement, too, there is room for debate.

A lawyer who cannot argue both sides of any issue will very quickly find himself with only half a clientele.

God, country, Jesus, and the US News & World Report law school rankings, but not necessarily in that order.

There are two types of lawyers: the arrogant elitist snobs, and the ones who were too stupid to become arrogant elitist snobs.

Textualism: what the law says. Originalism: Thomas Jefferson's subjective feelings.

(A) A criminal law judge protects goodness from evil. (B) A criminal law judge protects clean people from trash. (C) A criminal law judge is a rich white man who has been given the authority to ruin poor black young men's lives by sending them to jail. Have I not just said the same thing three times from different points of view?

Rigid rules, unfettered discretion, or the unfathomable compromise somewhere in between?

The law is what a lawyer says it is until someone proves him wrong.

The first thing we do is we kill all the people who tell lawyer jokes that aren't really funny.

Legal writing should be written to be as strong as possible.

Make your legal writing strong.

MAKE your legal writing STRONG!

Be aggressively reasonable.

Go in, make your point, and get out. Don't narrate.*

Be entertaining but informative, for a jury.

Persuasive public speaking, legal research, or technology: win in at least two of these three areas to win at trial.

Never make opposing counsel's argument for them.*

Never say never. Never say always.*

Be aggressively honest and assert the truth even to your own detriment. Juries tend not to believe lawyers whom they view as dishonest.

A case opinion which does not enable a lawyer to predict future holdings on similar yet different facts, and which does not enable law-abiding citizens to predict whether they break or obey the law, is as ephemeral as a puff of smoke, and as dangerous to the health!

The Legal Realists say that a Judge rules based on what he ate for breakfast. This is true only if he ate for breakfast poison that shut down the language and cognitive function centers in his brain.

A multi-factor fact-specific balancing test? Oh, you mean just let the Judge do whatever he wants and do whatever his feelings tell him to do, right? Why not just say so?

A Partner has to succeed. An Associate has to avoid failure.

If the Associates are the exploited slaves of the Partners, they are the most well-compensated slaves in human history.

A great trial lawyer plans out in advance the inferences the jury will draw and when they will draw them.

The benefit to society of the legal profession should be measured by what happens to people who hire bad attorneys. (Hint: what happens is they get a trove of horrors when their lawyer messes up their case!)

Lawyers dance across the hot coals of legal uncertainty every day.

A client is paying his lawyer to be superhuman.

A trial is like an election. It's a popularity contest, high IQ is not always what wins, and sometimes people cheat.

The judge can do whatever he wants. Whether he is right or wrong to do it is another matter entirely.

The art of legal writing is the art of making arguments to a judge who is too busy to consider your arguments. As such, what you say does not matter, but what you seem to have said is all-important.

What does it mean in legal doctrines to say that something must be "reasonable", such as the reasonable expectation of privacy for the Fourth Amendment, reasonable expectations in contract law, or reasonable precautions in torts? "Reasonable" either means nothing or else it means everything. It means not too much and not too little and whatever standard of measurement is asserted as the truth for measuring too much and too little—ah, but how to measure is nothing or everything!

*These I must attribute to various friends and/or my past law professors.

READING LIST

Also by this author:
What They Won't Tell You About Objectivism
Golden Rule Libertarianism
XYAB Economics
The Apple of Knowledge
The Golden Wand Trilogy
Project Utopia
The Office of Heavenly Restitution
Rob Seablue and the Eye of Tantalus
The Prince, The Girl, and The Revolution

ABOUT THE AUTHOR

Russell Hasan lives and works in the United States. He is a lawyer, philosopher, novelist, amateur software developer, sports fan, and gamer, among other things. More information about him can be found at russellhasan.com.

Made in the USA
Middletown, DE
29 January 2020

83890626R00019